If it don't make
DOLLARS
it don't make

CENTS

UnCommon Cents

Bishop Charles
A. Messenger

If it don't make Dollars
It don't make Cents

Un₵ ommon ₵ents

Bishop Charles A. Messenger

If it Don't Make Dollars it Don't Make Cents

Bishop Charles A. Messenger
Rewrite by M. F. Cage
Published by PurTeaching Publishing
www.purteachingpub.com
Minnesota

All Scripture quotations, unless otherwise indicated, are taken from the Holy Bible, King James Version or New King James®.

ISBN - 978-0-615-42522-1

Some people write out of their experiences while others write what they have experienced. Both perspectives are refreshing and provide revelatory insight. Over the years I have read books and articles that capture both perspectives but none in the refreshing way that this body of work has been presented. It is not often that you can read a book that teaches a known truth that is presented with authenticity and anointing. When asked to read this work I was somewhat reluctant because of my schedule but when I picked it up to browse through it several things caught my eye which prompted me to take a more serious look at this work.

Dr. Charles Messenger has done a masterful job in addressing a subject in the scripture that is most controversial in our contemporary times. He seems to have a way of putting the message of financial prosperity in common sense terms with infallible scriptural proof. I am so very proud of his unique and uncanny presentation of this faith teaching which can withstand the scrutiny of the critical eye. This book is yet another confirmation that God has no respecter of persons in that He has revealed to Dr. Messenger a refreshing approach to a plethora of financial faith principles. Bishop Messenger is practical in his approach because he is simply sharing the experiences of his journey to financial prosperity.

This book will challenge you to look at God's plan for kingdom giving and receiving in a new way. It will also expand your understanding on how to be "Mo" blessed which is a chapter that challenges you to take the step into disciplined giving that yields supernatural results. This chapter is a must read for every saint to anchor themselves in the powerful truth on systematic giving. I recommend this book without any reservations because if God can bring the Messengers to millionaire status by these faith principles He can do it for you. This is truly a good read that will give you the scriptural shove into the dynamic life of living by your giving!

Prologue

First of all I would like to give thanks to Doctor Loyace Foreman, Jr. and the New Vision Family for believing in me. I appreciate your faith efforts to partner with me by transcribing and provoking thought. This will be a momentous word for the benefit of the body of Christ. Thank you for stirring my gift enough to author this book. I value everything you did tremendously.

Content

Uncommon Mindset
Transformational Thinking 13

Operating in Faith 29

The Secret to Getting 43

How to Give Money You Don't Have 63

Becoming Mo' Blessed 79

Kunta vs. Tobi 97

Practical Examples of Wealth Creation
and Money Management 111

INTRODUCTION

God gave me a series of messages concerning how to turn a setback into a comeback. It was in these messages that God showed me how to turn different areas of human life around for the better. He showed me how to turn things around emotionally, physically, financially and in other life areas. Many of us have had setbacks in different ways, and didn't know how to recover, particularly in the area of finances.

Rather than making a comeback, many of you stay financially stuck year after year. You have too much debt, not enough income, and no relief in sight. So today I want to help you deal with the setbacks in your life, particularly in the area of finances. I want to expose you to what I call "Uncommon Cents." Some people reading this may not have experienced a financial setback; for those people, I believe this teaching will help you avoid one.

Uncommon Cents is a term that has a twofold meaning. First of all, it describes the uncommon wealth that God has allowed my wife and me to accumulate. Second, it represents the Uncommon Cents that we operate by in order to attract, sustain, and manage this uncommon wealth. God is interested in showing His people how to make a comeback.

It's no sin to get knocked down and fall in the mud, but it is a sin when you stay down in the mud. God wants you to pick yourself up, dust yourself off, and start fighting again. God put the ability to fight in us because He knew we were going to need to fight in life. In the Bible, David attributes his strength to the Lord who "teacheth my hands to war."

A Psalm of David. Blessed be the LORD my strength, which teacheth my hands to war, and my fingers to fight. *(Psalms 144:1)*

You have to develop a fighting spirit. God knows that in order for you to get what He has for you, you're going to have to fight the good fight of faith. The enemy is not going to give you anything; if you're going to make a comeback, you have to take it. Pastor Vernon Johns said, "If you see a good fight, get in it."
This book will help stir up your fighting spirit.

You've got to declare, "I am a fighter." I love to fight, I came to fight, I'll start the fight, and I'm going to win the fight. You've got to stir yourself up. When some people give their life to the Lord, they get passive about important areas of their life. Truth is, when you're rolling with the Lord you can't be passive.

We don't roll like that; you have to be aggressive about this Kingdom work. The Word of God says that the Kingdom of God suffers violence and the violent take it by force. You have to get your taking spirit back. It's time to stir up your violent spirit. The Devil has taken somethings from you, and you have to let him know, "I'm gonna take em' back!" The Bible doesn't say Jesus *asked* the Devil for the "Keys to the Kingdom;" the Bible says He *took* them. So get ready to take the keys to your financial prosperity. If you've had a financial setback, it's time to start your comeback.

Uncommon Mindset
Transformational Thinking

For as he thinketh in his heart, so [is] he...

Proverbs 3:7

If you are going to have uncommon results, you need to begin by thinking uncommon thoughts. In order for you to have uncommon thoughts, you have to get rid of your
common mindset. The word of God tells us in
Romans 12:2, *"Be not conformed to this world,
but be ye [you] transformed by the renewing of
your mind."* Also, *Let this mind be in you, which
was also in Christ.*

God wants to transform your mind and

your way of operating so He can do the uncommon with you. He warns or charges us in His word not to be conformed to the world, not to operate like everyone else. When you operate like everyone else, you get the same result as everyone else. If you were to poll most people as to what their number one problem is in life, they would tell you—if they were honest—that they are broke (financially deprived). The reason why they, and so many others are broke is because they are operating by inferior thinking instead of superior knowing.

IMPREGNATION

My goal in this chapter is to get you pregnant. Yes, that's right, my goal is to get you pregnant—both male and female. Now before you write me off as some kind of crazed pervert, just hear me out. I want to get you pregnant with the things of God, and the good news is that God doesn't get people pregnant like we do. God gets you pregnant by His Spirit and His Word.

In Luke chapter one, the Angel came to Mary and told her that she was going to have a child, and Mary said, "How can this be, seeing that I know not a man." The Angel responded, "The Holy Ghost shall come upon thee," and that which shall be born of you shall be holy. My goal throughout this book, and particularly in this chapter, is to get you pregnant with God's word concerning your prosperity. It's time to have the power of the Holy Ghost come upon you to deliver the promised Abundant Life.

INFERIOR THINKING VS. SUPERIOR KNOWING

The system you have in place is perfectly designed to give you the result you are getting (poverty). If you are going to get different results, you have to change the system you are operating in. Most people have been limited to operating by what I call an "Inferior Thought Pattern." They have been operating by what they think, feel, and what others have told them. Many people are *thinking* they are doing the right thing, or what is necessary, but I want to show you there is a better way. I want to first start by asking you a simple question. How did you develop this inferior thinking? (Hmmm!)

There are four primary factors that shape our beliefs and our thinking process.

1. **Environment** - The things you see and the places you've been give you a picture or idea in your mind of how things should be. Your environment shapes your belief in what is possible. You need to be exposed to different places and experiences. The world is bigger than your neighborhood.

2. **Credible Others** - Things have been told to you by people whom you look up to—people like Momma n'em, family, teachers, and "Big People" (those you want in your life).

3. **Repetitious Information** -The mind is an information database; information comes in,

gets filed, and is retrieved and applied in relevant situations when needed. The mind is designed to accept the first information it receives, and repeated information has the potential to be accepted as truth, even if it isn't truth. Because you heard it over and over again, it has become truth for you. The sayings that you've heard, whether true or not, become part of your belief system. Clichés like "God don't like ugly," "Cleanliness is next to godliness," "Money is the root of all evil," and others, become part of our belief system and dictate our life responses. However, none of those clichés are in the word of God.

4. **Experience** – An experience makes the most potent impact in the lives of people. When I experience something that lines up with something I previously believed, the belief becomes reinforced in my mind. The ideas, thoughts, and concepts I've had in my mind now have even stronger evidence to support

something I hold as "true." If men repeatedly hurt you in your relationships, it may after a awhile believe that all men are dogs.

Now that you know the factors that go into developing your inferior thinking, you can decide to change them. When you change your inferior thinking, you will stop producing inferior results. These four factors have shaped us to operate in inferior thinking, but we can change the input we receive from these factors to operate by "Superior Knowing."

1. **Environment** – I need to plug into a Godly community of faith-filled believers (a church or fellowship) where the plain and thorough truth of the Word of God is taught.

2. **Credible Others** – I must learn how to allow the Word of God to become the most credible authority in my life; "If God's Word says it, that settles it." The word of God is the most credible source in this world. Also you have to allow a trustworthy Man or Woman of

God to pastor (feed me with knowledge, wisdom and understanding) my soul and understanding.

3. **Repetitious Information** – In order for the word to sink in and transform your mind, as according to Romans 12:2 "Be ye transformed by the renewing of your mind," I will have to hear it over and over again. Faith comes by hearing; and hearing, by the repeated word of God. This can be accomplished in two ways. First of all, it can be accomplished by regular attendance and participation in church. The second way is to become an avid listener of audio CDs or video DVDs of the messages taught by your minister or other like-minded ministers. Romans 10:17 states that faith comes by hearing; and hearing, by the word of God. So you have to listen to the word of God over and over again to change what you believe.

4. **Experience** - When I commit to regularly at-

tending a church and to allowing the word taught there to be the credible authority in my life--and I hear that word again and again--I will begin to have new experiences. Hearing the repeated word will cause you to do or live the word. These experiences will validate what God's word says you ought to do.

Again, the world system that is in place is perfectly designed to give you the result you are presently getting (poverty). Everywhere I look, people are saying they don't have enough money, they're struggling financially, and how broke they are. They are living an inferior life, and they're living this life because of their inferior thinking.

I want to show you a better way. You don't have to live by inferior thinking; you can choose to live by "superior knowing." Superior knowing comes from doing things God's way. God already knows the answer to every question and the solution to every problem. So you and I simply have to learn to plug into God and allow the information to download. The plan, or the strategy, and the right results will follow. God already knows the solution. God has already planned for your success and your prosperity.

For I know the thoughts that I think toward you, saith the LORD, thoughts of peace, and not of evil, to give you an expected end. *(Jeremiah 29:11)*

You and I must simply learn how to download the information from God. Let me assist you a little further. Most people think humans were born randomly, with no specific purpose or specific mission for their lives. That is not true; God designed you with a *specific* purpose and mission in mind. Jeremiah testifies to this.

Jeremiah 1:5 says, "Before I formed thee in the belly I knew thee; and before thou camest forth out of the womb I sanctified thee,

[and] I ordained thee a prophet unto the nations."

This passage clearly lets us know that God made us all with a specific purpose in mind. The truth of the matter is, you were fearfully and wonderfully made, and the Bible goes on to say that you were made for such a time as this. So God selected, molded, made, and chose to give you life at this time. Your thoughts, ideas and abilities are perfectly suited for life as it occurs today.

Just imagine God creating you or bringing you into being 300 years ago as an African-American person; you would probably have neither the physical stamina nor the mental temperament to endure slavery. Having someone tell you what to do all the time, living in subhuman conditions, and being beaten or punished whenever you didn't please your master would have been too much for you to bear. You would have snapped off and made the master or the overseers shoot you. Working in the sweatshops of the industrial era also would have proved to be too grueling for many of us. You were designed for this technology-dependent, microwave-ready, information-driven society that we live in now. You were created for such a time as this.

God is doing a new thing and, contrary to popular belief, God is always up to something new. The problem is, every time God introduces something new, we react like the Water Boy's (Bobby Bouche') mother, and we don't recognize it as from God; we accuse the advancement of being from "The Devil."

When God gave man the idea of the TV, the church said it was the devil. When God gave man the idea for the computer, the church again responded, it's the devil. Our problem is, every time God tries to bless His church with the next witty idea and invention that He promised us in Malachi chapter 3, we (the church) take a pass, accusing those things as being of the devil. As a result, the billions of dollars that God desire to go to the church are received by the world instead.

The wealth transfer that God has designed for His people is yours when you understand and receive the revelation of His word. *Proverbs 13:22 says, "The wealth of the sinner is laid up for the just."*

The wealth that God has purposed for you is in fact being blocked by you. So rather than the church receiving and benefiting financially from the witty ideas that God is desiring to transfer to us, many people choose to struggle, scrounge and scrape to get by. It's time to break that way of thinking and embrace God's principles and precepts for prosperous living.

FAITH SUMMARY

Most people want a better lifestyle or an easier path. Yet you must be willing to do what it takes to get it. Fact is, God desire to get in the fight with you and make your dreams come to pass more than you can imagine. However, in order for you to start moving in a more faithful direction you have to transform the way you think. When you actively start focusing your attention in the four areas that shape belief - Environment, Creditable Others, Repetitious Information, Experience; you will see the hand of God move more and more in your life. When you are obedient to God's way of operating then and only then can the wealth transference take place.

Here is the wisdom; I said all that to say this. Humpty Dumpty sat on the wall, Humpty Dumpty had a great fall. All the king's horsemen and all the king's men could not put Humpty back together again. My question is, why did they go to the kings horsemen or the kings men? Why didn't they just go to the King.

When you are operating in inferior thinking you depend on <u>resource</u> rather than the <u>source</u>. God is not thinking of a plan for you. That is inferior thinking. Superior knowing- Jeremiah 29.11 - For I know the thoughts that I think toward you, saith the LORD, thoughts of peace, and not of evil, to give you an expected end. *Why do you keep going to NA, AA, AAA, Dr Phil, Cleo, Oprah, and momma nem? Why not just go to the*

Word of God? John 1.1 - In the beginning was the Word, and the Word was with God, and the Word was God.

Operating in Faith

Now faith is the substance of things hoped for,
the evidence of things not seen.
Hebrews 11:1

Everything that we obtain from God, we obtain by faith. Believe it or not, God does not respond to our *need*; He responds to our *faith*. I know this might mess with your theology, but the Scripture supports this over and over again. In Matthew 9:27-29, two blind men come to Jesus asking Him to heal them. Let's see what happened.

And when Jesus departed thence, two blind men followed him, crying, and saying, [Thou] Son of David, have mercy on us. And when he was come into the house, the blind

men came to him: and Jesus saith unto them,

Believe ye that I am able to do this? They said

unto him, Yea, Lord. Then touched he their eyes,

saying, According to your faith be it unto you.

Matthew 9:27-29

Jesus didn't just heal these blind men; He first asked them if they believed He could. Then he told them, "According to [their] faith it would done unto [them]." In other words, Jesus was not going to heal them just because they had a need, he healed them according to the level of faith they were operating in.

Likewise, The Gospel of Mark and Luke tell of the accounts of a man who was paralyzed with the palsy, and four of his friends carried him to a revival where Jesus was ministering. When they arrived there was no room in the building, and even the doorways were blocked by the crowd. Most people would have given up and turned around, but not these men of faith. Rather than giving up, they became more determined; in fact, they climbed up on the roof and tore a hole in it. Then they lowered their friend down into the meeting. The Scripture says that "When Jesus saw <u>their faith,</u>" He healed him.

We can see from these passages that Jesus responded to the situation based on their faith, not just because the paralyzed man needed to be healed. There is another passage of Scripture that also shows us how important faith is in getting God to move in your situation: Matthew 13:54-58, where Jesus had gone home to His home country. In verse 58 Jesus did not do many mighty works there because of their unbelief or lack of faith. Again, God is not a God who responds to need, but He is a God who responds to faith. If you want God to move in your situation, you must become a student of faith. You have to learn how to use the tools God has given you to live the way He purposed for you.

USING YOUR FAITH

Let me share with you several other key truths about faith and how to use it. Everybody is using his/her faith for something.

As I said in the last section, God is a God who responds to faith. And since we all want God to do something for us, we are using our faith to get those things. We may be using our faith for different things, but we all are using our faith in some way. So what we've got to do is to learn to respect the process of faith so we can get our needs met. Don't get hung up on what others are using their faith for; you just learn how to use yours.

For example, some of you may be using your faith for a husband, and that's good. Some of you may be using your faith for a wife, and that's good, too. But I'm not using my faith for either one of those, you know why? First of all, I'm not using my faith for a husband because I don't like men like that. Secondly, I'm not using my faith for a wife because I already have one. That brings me to my next point.

We use our faith for things that we don't have. The word of God says in Hebrews 11:1: Now faith is the substance of things hoped for, and the evidence of things not seen.

Faith is the substance of <u>hope</u> and the evidence of invisible things. I use my faith to get God to give me what I don't have yet [hoping for] and to bring into manifestation the dreams and desires I have that can't be seen outwardly but are only in my imagination.

Understanding "Now Faith."

Again, Hebrews 11:1 says:

Now faith is the substance of things hoped for, the evidence of things not seen.

For a minute I just want us to focus on those first three words of this passage: *"Now faith is..."* This is a very powerful revelation you must understand before we move on. Not really comprehending these words here might be what have been standing in the way of your faith victories. We've already established that God is moved by our faith; it is not our need that moves God but our faith, right? If what we are believing God for is always some future event--one of these old days, someday, when the time is right--then we are delaying God from moving.

As long as you keep your hope and expectation in the future, you are not exercising Now Faith. Just like Jesus said to the blind men, God through His Word is speaking to us According to your faith, now. You will receive from God "Now," not in the future; I will move on your behalf what you believe me for, right now. If you don't believe it right now, you have to increase your faith for right now when you ask.

The Bible teaches that faith comes by hearing; and hearing, by the word of God. If I want to elevate my level of believing in a certain area, what I need to do is increase hearing [reading, listening, and speaking] God's word in that given area.

WE NEED TO BE INSTRUCTED IN FAITH

In Luke 17, Jesus is discussing with the disciples the challenge that we have as human beings when others offend us. In verse 4 he alarms the disciples when he tells them to forgive their brother seven times a day if he asks for it.

Take heed to yourselves: If thy brother trespass against thee, rebuke him; and if he repent, forgive him. And if he trespass against thee seven times in a day, and seven times in a day turn again to thee, saying, I repent; thou shalt forgive him. And the apostles said unto the Lord, Increase our faith. *(Luke 17:3-5)*

Verse 5 records their response: "And the apostles said unto the Lord, Increase our faith." Jesus replied to them in verse 6, "And the Lord said, if ye had faith as a grain of mustard seed, ye might say unto this sycamine tree, "Be thou plucked up by the root, and be thou planted in the sea; and it should obey you." The disciples/apostles ask Jesus to increase their faith, and he teaches them [instructs them] by a parable. My assignment is to be a faith teacher and to instruct the Body of Christ on how to use your faith to complete your calling and get things you need and want.

FAITH FOR THINGS

A controversial topic that comes up within the church community is using faith to obtain things [material things]; people have a problem with believers pursuing material goods that don't necessarily pertain to religion. As long as we use our faith for healing or deliverance, people are ok with that. Yet when you decide to use your faith for things like money, a nicer house or a nice car, that's when the haters show up, even within the Body of Christ. People start talking about you and saying that you are misusing or are misguided in your faith efforts.

Well, I have two answers for them. First, it's better that I use my holy faith for things than for unholy means. I haven't always been saved, and you haven't either. You and I were getting things when we were in the world. I used to get my things through selling drugs, running after-hour joints, and from the con game.

Some of you used to get things by robbing, stealing, or by some other hustle. However, we got those things we liked that were outside of what we needed. And what I want to teach you is that God is okay with you having things outside of what you need as long as those things don't corrupt your Godly character.

Many people don't want you to use your faith for things; maybe they're deeply sincere

and well-meaning people who are just misin-
formed about the will of God. They will even
use the Bible to convince you that using faith
for stuff is wrong. One commonly misunder-
stood scripture is Matthew 6:25-32. This passage of scripture repeatedly uses the phrase
"Take no thought;" then it goes on to tell us to
take no thought for food, drink, or clothes, for
these are the things that worldly people pur-
sue.

> *Therefore I say unto you, Take no thought*
> *for your life, what ye shall eat, or what ye*
> *shall drink; nor yet for your body, what ye*
> *shall put on. Is not the life more than meat,*
> *and the body than raiment? Behold the*
> *fowls of the air: for they sow not, neither*
> *do they reap, nor gather into barns; yet*
> *your heavenly Father feedeth them. Are ye*
> *not much better than they? Which of you*
> *by taking thought can add one cubit unto*
> *his stature? And why take ye thought for*
> *raiment? Consider the lilies of the field,*
> *how they grow; they toil not, neither do*

they spin: And yet I say unto you, That
even Solomon in all his glory was not ar-
rayed like one of these. Wherefore, if God
so clothe the grass of the field, which to-
day is, and tomorrow is cast into the oven,
shall he not much more clothe you, O ye of
little faith? Therefore take no thought, say-
ing, What shall we eat? or, What shall we
drink? or, Wherewithal shall we be
clothed? (For after all these things do the
Gentiles seek) <u>*for your heavenly Father*</u>
<u>*knoweth that ye have need of all these*</u>
<u>*things*</u>*. But seek ye first the kingdom of*
God, and his righteousness; and all these
things shall be added unto you.

Matthew 6:25-33

This may confuse you or get you believing
that God doesn't want His children or His people to have things. Yet you have to understand
what this scripture is really saying. First of all,
the phrase "take no thought" comes from the
Greek word, "Merimnao" pronounced *me-ray-*

na-o which means not to be anxious or not to worry. So the scripture isn't telling us not to think about things or not to want things. It is telling us not to **worry** about whether or not we will get the things we need.

Instead of worrying, we need to trust God to provide for us. Matthew 6:33 tells us that if we seek God's way He will gives us all the things the world worries about: "But seek ye first the kingdom of God [Learn **the way God** would have you obtain these things], and his righteousness; and all these things shall be added [given] unto you." God doesn't mind you have things; He just doesn't want things to have you.

FAITH SUMMARY

Faith is the key that believer's use to bringing what is in the spirit realm into their natural realm. Faith was meant to be used to get things we don't have. When you understand "Now Faith," it empowers you to work your faith more effectively in your life and ministry. Most of all, faith is not automatic. We need to be instructed in faith so that our ability to manifest the things of God increases.

Faith cometh by hearing, by hearing and hearing and hearing, and hearing... I was not saved and I heard the word that Jesus was a Savior, faith came and I got saved. I was sick, and I heard the word that Jesus was a healer, faith came and I got my kidney. I was on drugs but when I heard the word that Jesus was a deliverer, faith came and I got delivered. I was broke and I heard the word that Jesus became poor that through his poverty I might become rich, faith came and I became a millionaire.

You can't have faith for something you haven't heard the word about, because faith cometh by hearing and hearing and hearing. The promises of God are received by faith. Faith is released by the words of my mouth. There is a knowledge above college, and that is the word of God.

The Secret to Getting

While the earth remaineth, seedtime and harvest, and cold and heat, and summer and winter, and day and night shall not cease.

Genesis 8:22

Becoming a Giver

Bring ye all the tithes into the storehouse, that there may be meat in mine house, and prove me now herewith, saith the LORD of hosts, if I will not open you the windows of heaven, and pour you out a blessing, that there shall not be room enough to receive it.

(Malachi 3:10)

The way to prosperity and being financial

blessed comes through Giving. The Bible tells us time and time again that financial blessing comes as a result of our ability to give.

The book of Malachi teaches us that when we give a Tithe and Offering, God will open the windows of Heaven and pour us out a blessing [so great] that you and I can't even [contain it]. Most believers know this scripture but don't understand the value of the principle being taught. Also consider the passages below:

Give, and it shall be given unto you; good measure, pressed down, and shaken together, and running over, shall men give into your bosom. For with the same measure that ye mete withal it shall be measured to you again. *(Luke 6:38)*

Many people pray and ask God to make them a giver; God replies He can't. It's true, child of God, God cannot make you or me a giver. He simply commands us to give, and the way we become a giver is to just do what Luke 6:38 says: "Give."

The second reason some people have problems giving is because they make all kinds of excuses why they cannot or should not give. Excuses like, "I'm too broke; I can't afford to give." Truth is, you can't afford not to give. Also I've heard, I would, but I don't know what they are doing with the money around here. [Side note – who are "they" anyway; and where is the "around here?" Are we talking about the Pastor and the Church, your spiritual leadership and your faith community? If you can't trust your Pastor and your Church Leadership, it's time to get out of that church and find somewhere where you can trust the Leadership.]

Now back to my point. The only way to become a giver is by giving, and you and I have to develop a [here it goes again] "Different mindset." You've got to understand that it is God who commands you to give, and that command is not conditionally based on other factors. God blesses us financially, and God commands us to give. Then God promises to bless us with more because of our obedience and faithfulness in the principle of giving. If you want to receive the financial blessing of the Lord, you need to become a giver.

RULES FOR GIVING

Now let me share with you some of the rules for giving. You can't give somebody something until you first pay them what you owe them. Let me give you an example. If you previously owed me $80, and were currently in need of another $30, why would I give you more? This system puts you in greater debt to me. Once you pay me what you owe me, then we can talk about me giving you more. This applies to God as well.

You can't give God something until you first pay God what you owe Him. I hear you thinking, "What do I owe God?" I'm glad you asked. I'm going to show you how God's economy works, and then it's up to you to pay God what you owe Him. When you receive the revelation, start giving so you can flourish in God's economy.

PAY YOUR DEBT, THEN GIVE YOUR GIFT

You owe God the Tithe. Tithe is a Hebrew word that means tenth. In Malachi 3, God commands us to bring the Tithe (a tenth part of your gross increase) unto Him (The Church). God's economy is set up on a sliding fee scale. God is basically saying, to each of us, you owe me 10 percent of your income/increase as rent. You owe God rent for staying on His planet, breathing His air, basking in His sunlight, etc. God says you owe me, and every time you get paid or receive any increase, you need to pay me.

Some people challenge the validity of tithing today; some of them try to say that tithing is an Old Testament rule that was under the Law, but now we are under grace. I appreciate your desire to be a good student of spiritual things, but if that's your thinking, you've missed two vital teachings in biblical scripture that you need to know. Get your Bible and turn to Genesis chapter 14, and let's look at verses 18 -20.

And Melchizedek king of Salem brought forth bread and wine: and he was the priest of the most high God. And he blessed him, and said, Blessed be Abram of the most high God, possessor of heaven and earth: And blessed be the most high God, which hath delivered thine enemies into thy hand. And he gave him tithes of all. *(Genesis 14:18-20)*

This is a story of an event in Abraham's life. The patriarch gave to Melchizedek the priest of the Most High God. This text clearly states that Abraham gave "Tithe" to Melchizedek. This event took place before the "Law" was given to Moses. So tithing was before the

Law. The second principle you need to understand comes from the "Law of Grace."

$$\mathbb{C}$$

**Moreover the law entered, that the offence
might abound. But where sin abounded,
grace did much more abound.**

(Romans 5:20)

The scripture says where the Law did
abound, Grace abounded more. This means
that God stepped His game up from the Law to
Grace through Jesus Christ. God's first attempt to establish for Himself a righteous people was through the "Law" of Moses, "The Ten
Commandments."

The Law set a standard for righteous living and, unfortunately, that standard could not
be met by human beings. Then God sent His
Son Jesus to be a ransom for all the law-
breakers and establish their righteousness
through Grace. God stepped His game up, so
where the Law only went so far in an attempt

to establish our righteousness, Grace went that much further to actually establish us (Believers) as the "Righteousness of God" through Jesus Christ. Just as God stepped His game up from the Law to Grace, you and I also need to step our game up from whatever we were commanded to do in the Law, or under the Law, that we ought to do even more Under Grace. So if under the law you paid 10 percent for rent, you ought to be paying at least 11 percent for rent under Grace.

Let me tell some of my personal testimony on how my wife and I operate in the Lord and the "mo' blessed" state in which we live. I want to remind you that my testimony is that God made me and my wife millionaires. I am not trying to brag; it's just a fact. God made us millionaires, and he did it by opening the windows of Heaven, bringing the blessing, and allowing us to harvest the hundred-fold returns on the Offerings and Seed that we brought to Him. An often overlooked part of Malachi 3 is its distinct mention of tithes *and offerings.*

Here's the order of our giving: I first pay my debt (Tithes), and then I prepare my offering and seed with the help of the Holy Spirit.

Going back to Grace abounding much more; my wife and I decided that just as grace abounded from God in every area of our lives-- in health, in deliverance, in promotion–that we would operate the same in our giving. We believed that the legal (according to the law) debt payment was 10 percent, so we were going to set our offering (grace giving) at 10 percent. Yep, that's right; we decided to make our offerings at least equal to our tithe (a total of 20 percent). To give God 20 percent is our way of thanking Him for all the great things He has done in our life. It is a small token of our appreciation. This is the simple secret to our financial success.

Most people lose their faith fight between seed time and harvest. God promises in Genesis 8 that as long as the earth remains that there would be seedtime and harvest-time. We have been sowing seeds in the Lord (His

Church) for more than 25 years now, and God has prospered us over and above. We operated by faith (according to God's Word), and God did what He promised. He has blessed us exceedingly, abundantly above.

We use these principles in our personal life but also in our ministry. In our ministry we tithe and sow into other ministries. Each month we give a tithe-offering to our Pastor's ministry and to other ministries. Now before you write me for an offering, understand that we only sow where God leads us, and not where people plead from us. As a result, we live an incredible life. Our church building is paid for; our Men's Restoration House, paid for; my wife's and my house is paid for; and our children's houses, paid for. Again, I'm not trying to brag. I'm just trying to show you what God will do if you learn to operate by these "Uncommon" ways of thinking and being.

God's word testifies that He is not a respecter of persons (Acts 10:34). God didn't do this for us just because He liked us; God did this for us because we learned to operate by His principles and precepts. Child of God, when you learn to operate by His principles and precepts, He'll do the same for you.

Tithing and offering weren't set up to benefit God. He doesn't need money to live, move and have His being. It was set up to benefit us (The Believers and His Church). God desires us to operate in these principles because He knows that seedtime always precedes harvest. God has laid out the principles, precepts and laws that must be followed on this earth in order for us to navigate successfully through life. You can't reap a harvest from God until you first sow some seed.

Too many people come to church looking for a blessing, but they haven't sown anything into His church or into His man/woman for God to bless. The only way that these types of people get blessed is from some other sowers overflow. Rather than getting their own blessing, they settle for the *crumbs that fall from the Master's Table.* Sure, you can get on the world's fast track to success and hopefully save enough money to make you feel secure. What you don't understand is, though God blesses the believers with money, it is not our true blessing. *He* is our exceeding great reward. When you don't tithe, the Bible says that you are a "God Robber." That means you stole God's tithe.

If you think about it, many people are driving stolen cars; some people in church are dressed in stolen clothes; and some of them are even wearing stolen hair and nails. What would happen if we treated our landlords, our mortgage holders, or our car finance companies the way we treat God (Hmmm)? You know, if we got right and brought all our stolen stuff and gave everything back to God, the church would need a much bigger offering basket.

GIVING: A HEART ISSUE

Contrary to popular belief, giving is not a pocket or purse issue. Believe it or not, giving is not really a money issue; it is a heart issue or a love issue. Matthew 6:21 just comes right out and says it: *For where your treasure is, there will your heart be also.*

John 3:16, which is probably one of the most widely known scriptures in the world, re-inforce the connection between giving and the heart. *"For God so loved the world that he gave his only begotten Son, that whosoever shall be-lieve in him should not perish, but they shall have everlasting life."* God so loved that he gave. Love is expressed through our giving of what is valuable and precious to us. When I give that which is precious to someone else, I communicate how much I value (love) that per-son. If we looked at your checkbook or your credit card statement, it would tell us clearly what you love and value.

As we examine the expenses, I am sure we'd find rent or mortgage and utilities pay-ments because you love or greatly value living indoors. We'd find a few grocery store entries, probably a couple of Wal-Mart, Target, or Sam's Club purchases because you love to eat and keep your home filled with useful supplies. We may find other lifestyle expenses like Pizza Hut, shoe stores, the barbeque joint, Blockbuster rentals or movie tickets, clothing store and cellular phone payments, etc. You get the picture. We love the ability to consume, consume, consume in our instant-gratification lifestyles. Don't get me wrong; I'm not hating on your lifestyle. I'm just trying to point out that we spend money on the things we love or to maintain the lifestyle we love. Also, I hope that your spouse, children, or other loved ones found their way into that list.

"Where your treasure is, that is where your heart is also." This could also be said another way: where your treasure goes, your heart will follow. One of the key ways we express our love is through spending our money and resources on people and things we value. Think back to when you were dating. If you're still dating you don't have to think back too far (LOL). You communicate your love through spending money to buy gifts or go places together. You may have bought flowers, candy, clothing, cologne and movie tickets. You went to fancy, expensive restaurants that you couldn't afford, and couldn't pronounce the items on the menu. The food was probably not as good as the chicken, ribs, or hamburger place around the way, but the sheer cost said I love or value you!

That same approach works with God. When you consistently bring your Tithes (pay God what you owe) and offerings (the amount beyond your tithe), you are communicating how much you love and value God. Just like at the fancy restaurant, the more you spend (give to God and the Kingdom), the more you communicate how much you love God. Of course, this is just one way of communicating your love, but it is one that is common among man. Your offering communicate how much you love God, because the tithe is already his.

DOING BIG THINGS WITH SMALL NUMBERS

The power in my ministry, Antioch Christian Center, is not that we have such a large number of members, but that our membership is made up largely of people who are givers. The majority of our people are tithers, offerers, sowers, and just outright generous givers. We are able to do more with 200-300 members than many churches with 2,000-3,000 members. While their members are still putting a dollar in the offering basket, our members are sowing their best seed every chance they get.

As leaders, my wife and I moved our giving up, and many of our members did likewise. We began to offer as much as we tithe, and they did the same. I believe that old saying that is supported by so many passages of scripture, "You can't beat God giving no matter how you try." Luke 6 says, "**Give** and **it shall be given [back]** unto you good measure, pressed down, shaken together, and running over. Mark 10:29-30 tells us that the **things we give for the gospel's (church's) sake** shall be multiplied back to us one hundredfold. Malachi 3 tells us that a reward for **faithful**

tithers and offering givers is that they shall receive a <u>blessing so great</u> they <u>won't have room enough to receive it</u>.

The faithfulness of our members in the area of giving has caused them to experience a "mo' blessed" state of being. Not only have we been able to do great things within the ministry, like pay off all our facilities, but by being "mo' blessed," we give a lot back to the community. Each year on Easter we give away Easter baskets to children; every summer we host a free barbeque picnic complete with ribs, chicken, burgers and all the sides and fixings; and on Thanksgiving we have a turkey giveaway. That's what I mean by "**mo' blessed**," not just enough for you and yours, but **enough to be a blessing to others**, and **still have something left over**.

FAITH SUMMARY

The Secret to Getting isn't really a secret at all. These faith principles have been around for centuries. Its simply become a giver. When you understand the rules to giving and develop a heart for giving, then you will experience getting at a new level. The tithe is the foundation but the offering and the seed causes a harvest that you won't have room to receive.

If you ask people how they are doing, most of them say, "I'm blessed and highly favored." What do you mean sister Flapjack? I'm blessed because I got a car, I got a house, I got my daughter kids out the system. Here's the lesson, she was blessed based on what she got. Acts 20.35 teaches us, that it is more of a blessing to give than to receive. So I taught our church how to be more blessed. We are now in a position to give the house , give the car, give the T.V. The Mo' Blessed person is the one putting something in the tin cup, not the one holding it. We will talk more about that later.

How to Give Money You Don't Have

Thou shalt make thy prayer unto him, and he shall hear thee, and thou shalt pay thy vows. Thou shalt also decree a thing, and it shall be established unto thee: and the light shall shine upon thy ways.

Job 22:27-28

When thou vowest a vow unto God, defer not to pay it; for he hath no pleasure in fools: pay that which thou hast vowed. Better is it that thou shouldest not vow, than that thou shouldest vow and not pay.

Ecclesiastes 5:4-5

JACOB'S VOW

These scriptures refer to a Biblical Principle known as *vowing and paying.* It is a principle I consistently use in my own life. Hear how this principle works. When people desire something from God, they come to the Lord in prayer, in worship, or even during a time of motivational giving and make a vow to give money, wealth, or some other valuable things they don't currently have in exchange for something they desire.

In Genesis 28 we see Jacob working this principle. At this point in his life, Jacob is a fugitive. He has swindled his brother Esau out of his birthright, and Esau is out to kill him. So Jacob is on the run for his life, and he ends up in a city called Luz, where he rests for the night. While he sleeps that night, he has a dream of a ladder in this place that stretches from Earth up to Heaven. On this ladder there are Angels ascending and descending, going back and forth between Heaven and Earth, and he hears the voice of God speaking from the top of the ladder. The voice of God is promising to bless Jacob and fulfill His Promise to Abraham through him.

And he dreamed, and behold a ladder set up on the earth, and the top of it reached to heaven: and behold the angels of God ascending and descending on it. And, behold, the LORD stood above it, and said, I am the LORD God of Abraham thy father, and the God of Isaac: the land whereon thou liest, to thee will I give it, and to thy seed; And thy seed shall be as the dust of the earth, and thou shalt spread abroad to the west, and to the east, and to the north, and to the south: and in thee and in thy seed shall all the families of the earth be blessed. And, behold, I am with thee, and will keep thee in all places whither thou goest, and will bring thee again into this land; for I will not leave thee, until I have done that which I have spoken to thee of.   *Genesis 28:12-15*

When Jacob awoke he had a dreadful feeling, having experienced the presence of God

Bishop Charles A. Messenger

in His dream. He then took the rock he had
used for a pillow and made a pillar (a monu-
ment of reverence to the Lord), and there–with
no money, no possessions, and with even his
life in jeopardy--he makes a vow to the Lord.

**And Jacob vowed a vow, saying, If God will
be with me, and will keep me in this way
that I go, and will give me bread to eat, and
raiment to put on, So that I come again to
my father's house in peace; then shall the
LORD be my God: And this stone, which I
have set for a pillar, shall be God's house:
and of all that thou shalt give me I will
surely give the tenth unto thee.**

Genesis 28:20-22

POWER OF THE VOW

The power of the Vow is the power of the Word
– The Spoken Word itself is used as a ransom
for something desired. Let's examine this
scripture to reinforce your understanding.
In the beginning God created. How did God

create? He created by the Word of His Mouth!

In the beginning was the Word, and the Word was with God, and the Word was God. The same was in the beginning with God. All things were made by him; and without him was not anything made that was made.

(John 1:1)

And God said, Let there be light, and there was light.   *Genesis 1:3*

And God said, Let there be a firmament in the midst of the waters, and let it divide the waters from the waters.   *Genesis 1:6*

And God said, let the waters under the heaven be gathered together unto one place, and let the dry [land] appear. And it was so. *Genesis 1:9*

In these three verses, and for the rest of the chapter, God is involved in the creation process. Everything God created, He created by speaking it into existence. The cadence repeated throughout the chapter is: God said let there be, and it was so. In verse 26, God put the frosting on creation by speaking man into existence.

And God said, Let us make man in our image, after our likeness, and let them have dominion over the fish of the sea, and over the fowl of the air, and over the cattle, and over all the earth, and over every creeping thing that creepeth upon the earth.   *Genesis 1:26*

Not only did God speak man into existence, He spoke man into existence to be like Him.

So God created man in his [own] image, in the image of God created he him; male and female created he them.   *Genesis 1:27*

So we can truthfully say that God created man with the ability to create our reality just like He created the reality of this world around us, by using the Spoken Word. My friend, God gave you and me the same creative power He has, the power of the spoken word. When we combine the power of the spoken word with God's system of financial blessing, "sowing and reaping," we have an unstoppable combination.

Vowing engages the creative power of speaking with the principles of giving, and it gives you the ability to create an offering in the spirit world for money or things that have not yet manifested in the natural. And at that moment, hear me well, and *at that moment* God gives me "credit" for the money I have not yet given.

In Gen 28 Jacob vows to bring God a tithe (a tenth part) of what he doesn't currently have. "But if thou will bless me, prosper me and bring me back safely, then I will make you my God and give you tithes of all." So here at Bethel, Jacob is a fugitive running for his life with nothing to offer; but, with his word, he makes a deal with God. Jacob's offer to God is that he will serve Him "if," God will bless him.

Jacob's service will be to recognize Him as his God and to bring God a tithe of what

God gives to him. I don't know how you inter-
pret that, but that sounds kind of like pimpin'
to me. Let me explain. Jacob is saying: God, I
don't have anything, and if you give me 100
percent of the blessings I desire, I will make
you my God and give you back 10 percent.
What kind of deal is that?

Don't get it twisted; you can't play God.
God set this system up to bless you when all
you have is your word. God will give you credit
for what you vow (speak into existence), but
God also holds you accountable to give what
you vowed you were going to give. The story of
Ananias and Sapphira in Acts 5 illustrates the
seriousness and the consequences of not keeping our vow to the Lord.

In Acts 4:32-37, we see a move of God in
the church to make sure that every believer
has sufficiency. Believers who owned possessions sold them and brought the proceeds to
the Apostles to build the church treasury and
to make sure poor believers didn't go without.
Ananias and Sapphira, a husband and wife, got

caught up in the mix. They vowed to sell their goods and bring all the proceeds to the Apostles like all the other believers. When they got the money, they thought it was too much to give. So they conspired between themselves to hold some back and to pretend to give it all. Let see what happened.

But a certain man named Ananias, with Sapphira his wife, sold a possession, And kept back part of the price, his wife also being privy to it, and brought a certain part, and laid it at the apostles' feet. But Peter said, Ananias, why hath Satan filled thine heart to lie to the Holy Ghost, and to keep back part of the price of the land? Whiles it remained, was it not thine own? and after it was sold, was it not in thine own power? why hast thou conceived this thing in thine heart? thou hast not lied unto men, but unto God. And Ananias hearing these words fell down, and gave up the ghost: and great fear came on all them that heard these things. And the young men arose, wound him up, and car-

ried him out, and buried him. And it was about
the space of three hours after, when his wife,
not knowing what was done, came in. And Pe-
ter answered unto her, Tell me whether ye sold
the land for so much? And she said, Yea, for so
much. Then Peter said unto her, How is it that
ye have agreed together to tempt the Spirit of the
Lord? behold, the feet of them which have bur-
ied thy husband are at the door, and shall carry
thee out. Then fell she down straightway at his
feet, and yielded up the ghost: and the young
men came in, and found her dead, and, carrying
her forth, buried her by her husband.
Acts 5:1-10

You see, my friend, God doesn't play with the vow. Just as you get credit for making a vow and eventually keeping it, you can pay severe consequences for breaking your vow. Now you probably won't drop dead, but God will be very displeased with you, and the return blessing that you were going to receive can be interrupted or cancelled. In the book of Ecclesiastes it plainly warns against this.

**Better is it that thou shouldest not vow,
than that thou shouldest vow and not pay.**

(*Ecclesiastes 5:5*)

FLIPPIN' THE SCRIPT (ON THE VOW)

This may seem like a spooky or weird concept to you, but it's something that you are familiar with. The credit card industry works under some of the same principles. The credit card system enables you to spend money you don't have. You simply pull out the plastic and get what you want, even if you don't have the money to pay for it. You make a vow **[give your word]** to the credit company that you will pay back the money you owe them. Up to this point, most of us have been successful in using the vow with the world to get into debt, anxiety, strife, and poverty. Why don't you try using this same vowing principle with God? It will make you blessed, Mo' blessed, and seriously prosperous like it did for me. Let me share with you an account from my own life.

MESSENGER'S LIFETIME VOW

Now that you understand the power of the vow, let me tell you about the vow I made that was the defining moment in my incredible journey to financial blessing. I told you before that when Debbie and I came to the Lord we were broke. We were more than $100,000 in debt and near foreclosure. I mean we had nothing; yet our blessing was there in the nothing state. Like Jacob, I made a vow unto the Lord: "Lord, if you will bless me, make me a millionaire, and make me the lender and not the borrower, then Lord I will bring you the first fruits of all my increase."

That day many years ago, I vowed (with nothing in my pockets) to give God the first pay check I made each year. And each year since then, no matter what has been happening in my finances, I bring that first check unto the Lord. I did my part, and God did His. He raised me up, made me a millionaire, and I lend and do not have to borrow.

The same God who did it for me is no respecter of persons, so if He did it for me, then He will do it for you. Amen! So now you know the secret of being able to give money that you don't have. No matter where you are, and no matter what you don't have, you do have the ability to *Make a Vow.*

FAITH SUMMARY

The Kingdom of God has many tools that the believer can use to walk out his/her faith. The power of the spoken word in a vow to the Lord can allow you to obtain credit with the Kingdom of God. Many patriarchs used the vow when they didn't have a sacrifice to offer. Learning how to use this tool in your faith walk will cause you to become more effective.

The way you give money you don't have is to make a vow or give your word. When you decree it or say it, it is established. Go takes you at your word. When Jacob made a vow or gave His word that he would give God a tithe if he could return to his land safely.

You got into debt by spending money you didn't have. They gave you the loan or credit card based on your word. Well, God is the same way. When you make a vow, God bless you before your pay what you owe based all on your word.

Becoming Mo' Blessed
Living in the More Blessed State

I have showed you all things, how that so labouring ye ought to support the weak, and to
remember the words of the Lord Jesus, how he
said, It is more blessed to give than to receive.

Acts 20:35

This passage of scripture is so powerful
and holds so much meaning for me, I can't
hardly wait to explain it. This has been my
mantra for years: "It is more blessed [Mo'
Blessed] to give than to receive." My wife Debbie and I have been preaching and teaching
how to become "Mo' blessed" for years now. If

you ask many Christians, they will tell you that they are blessed. If you ask them why, they normally will tell that they got something, and that thing they got validates why they are blessed. For example, "I got a new car; boy, I'm blessed;" or "I got a new house; I'm so blessed."

Most of us, as a rule, equate our blessings with getting something. Don't get me wrong, getting is good; as a matter of fact, it's a blessing. However, Acts 20:35 says that you and I don't have to settle for blessed, but we can be Mo' blessed. This passage teaches that we are Mo' blessed when we give. We are blessed when we get/receive, but we become Mo' blessed when we give. It's Mo' blessed to be in a position to give. In Genesis 12 God told Abraham, "I'm going to bless you to be a blessing so all the nations of the earth can be blessed by you."

Again, this is a mindset change. My desire was not to just be in position to get (be blessed). My desire was to have enough to give to others (be Mo' blessed). It takes more power to give than to receive; you are Mo' blessed when you are able to give to the tin cup than to hold out the tin cup trying to recieve. My prayer and desire has always been to have enough to be a blessing to others.

The beginning of Acts 20:35 illustrates what I am saying: "I have showed you all things, how that so labouring ye ought to *support the weak*." This illustrates my testimony of how, when I was weak [financially weak and in debt], someone labored to support me so I could become strong.

Years ago, in the very early years of our ministry, my wife and I were more than $100,000 in debt, and our house was in foreclosure. We were really weak financially. An older Jewish Lady was attending our church, and she knew our financial situation. She told us that God wanted to bring us out of the situation that we were in. We sure were excited to hear that, but what she said next didn't make sense to me at the time. She said that God wanted us to "Give our way out of debt."

You've got to understand we were less than zero, I mean we didn't have anything. Remember what Billy Preston said, "Nothing from nothing leaves nothing." How were we going to give our way out? We were broke as a joke; we were so broke that we couldn't pay attention. The lady told us again that God wanted us to give our way out. Then she did something totally unexpected, she gave me and my wife $1,000. This was the first time somebody ever gave $1,000 in the ministry. She did what the scripture said and "Supported our weakness." She put us in a position to give. Now came the test of whether we would become givers or not.

Once the $1,000 was in our hands, we had a choice to make. We could buy some new stuff. The Devil start telling me about all the bills I could pay, but we made the choice to give to the Lord. The first thing we did was to pay our tithes; then we gave a big offering to the ministry. God was testing us but, "Glory to Jesus," we passed. Many of you have been through that test, and some of you are going through that test right now. You got a big pay day, won a lawsuit, hit the lottery (LOL), and you said when it comes in I'm going to sow something into my church. Yet when the money gets into your hot hands you forgot your vow to God and your desires for the Lord and the church vanished. If you want a better life you have to do better.

FAITHFULNESS

Most people desire to rule over many before they have been faithful over a few. Your faithfulness qualifies you to rule over many. Here's the deal that God makes with us. When you are faithful and patient for your part, then I (God) will do my part. My part is to make you a ruler over many.

"...thou hast been faithful over a few things, I will make thee ruler over many things..."
(Matthew 25:21)

Faithfulness is right now. You are either faithful, or you are not. If you aren't faithful with what you've got now, you won't be faithful if God gives you more. If you are faithful now with the little you have, you will be faithful when God gives you more. **You have enough right now to show God you can be trusted with more.** You must become faithful at tithing $100 before you can be faithful about tithing $200, $300 or $500 dollars. Remember, "Now faith is;" "he that is faithful [now] **is faithful.**"

SUPERNATURAL VS. SUPER-NATURAL

You've got nothing to lose because you are, most likely, already financially weak and in debt. When you ask yourself, how did I get into this kind of debt, the answer is super-naturally. There are forces that operate outside of the ordinary, or the natural, that work to either increase or decrease us financially. The forces that work to increase us are Super-natural (spiritual laws and principles), that when properly operated will bring us out of debt and into prosperity. There are also super-natural forces (powers that work in extra ordinary ways) that work to keep us in debt.

SUPER-NATURAL DEBT

When I say that you got in debt super-naturally, what I mean is that you got into debt where there was a power present pulling you into debt or trying to keep you in debt faster than you could work to get out. I can hear many of you asking yourselves, "What is he talking about?" It's simple; the super-natural power working to keep you in debt is called "compound interest."

Here is how it works. Let's say you get a credit card and you charge $1,500 to buy something you like. The interest rate is 20 percent. The credit card company then sends you a bill with the minimum payment of $20 a month, to which you say, "That ain't bad." You can afford that, but you are only looking at one aspect of what is going on, the $20 dollar pay-

ment. What is going on "super-naturally" be-
hind the scene is this:

Principal (Original) Loan
    $1,500
Annual Compounding Interest (.20x1,500) =
<u>300</u>
Principal and Interest Year 1
    $1,800
Monthly Payments ($20 x 12 = 240)
-<u>240</u>
Total Debt at the end of Year 1 $1,560

This is if it goes perfectly, no late payments, no late charges, or other fees added to
your account. Let's go over it again. You bor-
rowed $1,500 day 1(when you got your stuff);
then you paid them $20 a month which is $240
for the year; they charged you interest of 20
percent ($300 for the $1,500 you spent); and at
the end of 12 months you owe more than you
did in the beginning $1,560. You see what I
mean when I say that you are being pulled in
faster than you can work your way out? You

got into a system that has been super-naturally designed to keep you in debt and financial bondage forever.

ESCAPING SUPERNATURALLY

You see you got in super-naturally (through a system that uses superior natural means to keep you in). I'm going to show you how to get out Supernaturally (with God's help) by tithing, offering, and sowing seeds into the Kingdom of God. The Bible tells us that when we sow into good ground we will reap 30, 60, even a one hundredfold harvest on that seed sown.

And other [seed] **fell on good ground**, and **did yield fruit** that sprang up and increased; and brought forth, some **thirty**, and some **sixty**, and some **an hundred**. (*Mark 4:8*)

It is the super-natural that keeps people in debt, and if we are going to come out of debt it's going to be done Supernaturally. God wants to pull you out like He pulled us out. In order to come out, you've got to follow His system. Remember, the system that you have in place is perfectly designed to get you the results you are getting.

Child of God, if you are going to come out, you have to change the system you sow into. The Kingdom of God has an established order and a regimen to bring us into financial blessing.

The first thing we must do to receive this blessing and walk in this order is to Tithe. Tithing puts God first. We bring God His 10 percent rent consistently (over and over again), and He promises to "open the Windows of Heaven to us and pour us out a Blessing." A lot of people think that means money, as if God is going to open Heaven's windows and rain down dollar bills. But it doesn't work exactly like that. When God opens the windows, He is opening places of opportunity, witty ideas, and invention that can bring you money, prosperity and increase.

Many times in the financial arena these are referred to as income streams, pipelines, and sources of cash-flow. That's why scripture says He will pour out a blessing that you won't have room enough to receive. You will have too many avenues, opportunities, and money-making ideas to take advantage of them all. Yet you will *have* to take advantage of them. Remember, God is not raining down money, but He is putting you in unique positions to bring in incredible amounts of wealth.

As believers we must not only tithe (pay our debt), we must also become givers, giving to God willingly of what we have left. In return for our offering, God's laws and principles will cause increased giving to come to us. Luke 6 says: it will be given to us in good measure, pressed down shaken together, and running over.

You must also become a seed sower. This may be somewhat foreign to you in your urban-ized modern society where we buy all our food at grocery stores versus growing it, but it is as simple as it sounds. If I want to receive a harvest, I must first sow (give, plant) some seed. The good news is that money is a seed that can be sown, and God promises a return on that investment of 30, 60, or even one hundredfold. There is also another unique quality of a money seed that is different from all other types of seeds, and that is that money has the ability to transform into whatever you command it to be. Ecclesiastes 10:9 reminds us that, "money answers all things" you need.

After you've tithed, offered, and sowed, you must learn how to reap. Reaping involves diligence and effort in working to bring in your harvest, walking through doors of opportunity, and following through on the witty ideas and inventions that God will give you. Too many people are sitting back waiting for God to prosper them. They don't understand that God is waiting for them. Joshua 1 makes this plain:

This book of the law shall not depart out of thy

mouth; but thou shalt meditate therein day and night, that thou mayest observe to do according to all that is written therein. For **then thou** shalt make **thy** way **prosperous,** and **then** thou shalt have **good** success.

Joshua 1:8

Your prosperity and success require you to do something to make it happen. The direction and instruction on what to do come from spending time with God in prayer, reading His Word, and being obedient to what he tells you to do. Your prosperity will be a direct result of the intimacy you have with God.

FOR CHURCHES AND CORPORATE VENTURES

The principles we are sharing don't just work for individuals; they work for churches, organizations, and even nations. There is an account of special giving in I Chronicles 29 that reveals the power and principle of corporate giving that accomplishes building of the Kingdom and brings blessings on everyone.

Furthermore David the king said unto all the congregation, Solomon my son, whom alone God hath chosen, is yet young and *tender, and the work is great: for the palace is not for man, but for the LORD God. Now I have prepared with all my might for the house of my God the gold for things to be made of gold, and the silver for things of silver, and the brass for things of brass, the iron for things of iron, and wood for things of wood; onyx stones, and stones to be set, glistering stones, and of divers colours, and all manner of precious stones, and marble stones in abundance. Moreover, because I have set my affection to the house of my God, I have of mine own proper good, of gold and silver, which I have given to the house of my God, over and above all that I have prepared for the holy house, Even three thousand talents of gold, of the gold of Ophir, and seven thousand talents of refined silver, to overlay the walls of the houses withal: The gold for things of gold, and the silver for things of silver, and for all manner of work to be made by the hands of ar-*

tificers. And who then is willing to consecrate his service this day unto the LORD? Then the chief of the fathers and princes of the tribes of Israel, and the captains of thousands and of hundreds, with the rulers of the king's work, offered willingly, And gave for the service of the house of God of gold five thousand talents and ten thousand drams, and of silver ten thousand talents, and of brass eighteen thousand talents, and one hundred thousand talents of iron. And they with whom precious stones were found gave them to the treasure of the house of the LORD, by the hand of Jehiel the Gershonite. Then the people rejoiced, for that they offered willingly, because with perfect heart they offered willingly to the LORD: and David the king also rejoiced with great joy. 1 Chronicles 29:1-9

In this account David demonstrates the practice known as "Motivational Giving." David had planned for the building of the house of God and over the years had stored many precious and necessary materials for the project.

Before he died, David rallied the nation to give toward this great effort. He motivated others to give by his personal giving. Verse 3 starts out with David saying it was because of his love for God that he began to prepare to build the Temple. But he did not give only what was in the treasury but also of his personal possessions: "I have of my own proper good[s], of silver and gold...given."

First, David gave us verse 3. Then in verse 6 the chiefs, princes, captains, and rulers gave, or "offered willingly." And in verse 9 the people gave, and everyone rejoiced because everyone offered willingly unto the work of the Lord. Then David acknowledges the blessing: that it is a blessing to be in relationship with the Living and True God. And he thanked God for blessing him and the nation with so much prosperity that they could give an offering like this to build a house for the Lord.

FAITH SUMMARY

How to become "Mo Blessed" is the next step in the believers salvation walk. Though many people like to be on the receiving end of blessings, the best position to be in is when you are the giver and not the borrower.

Also, the enemy has supernaturally stack the deck against you, and the only way you can come out of a life of overwhelming debt and death, you have to be faithful to God's principles and precepts to become a giver.

Kunta vs. Tobi

And hath made us kings and priests unto God
and his Father; to him be glory and dominion
for ever and ever. Amen.

(Revelation 1:6)

I want to start this chapter by reminding
you of a memorable scene from the TV miniser-
ies "Roots," based on the Alex Haley novel. If
you haven't seen the movie, I strongly recommend it. There is a particular scene where
Kunta Kinte, a descendant of African royalty, is
captured and enslaved. Kunta, played by Le-
Var Burton, is captured after refusing to identify himself as a slave and running to live the
life of a **"Free-man."** Upon his capture and re-

turn to the plantation, Kunta is immediately taken to the whipping post to be punished. The overseer's assistant immediately begins whipping Kunta to punish him for running away. Once Kunta has been thoroughly punished for his offense, the overseer begins what is commonly known as the "Breaking process" to get this royal African to accept a new identity—that of an American Slave. The devil wants you to accept this idea of American slave. Yet God wants you to know that He called you king and priest, and Jesus is that King of kings.

The overseer asks Kunta what is his name and, of course, he replies, "Kunta." At that, the overseer commands his assistant to give him several lashes. Again, he asks the question, "What is your name?" He replies once again, "Kunta." This series of questioning and answering takes place repeatedly, again and again (much easier for overseer than for Kunta) until, finally broken by fatigue, pain, and human frailty, Kunta responds, "My name is Toby." Kunta no longer identifies himself with his God-given king name of Kunta Kinte but accepts the identity of Toby, the slave.

In today's society, different systems have been set up to beat you into submission and cause you to become a slave to its system. The borrower always becomes slave to the lender. So ask yourself, are you Kunta the king or Toby the borrower/slave. The compound interest we talked about previously is set up to keep you a slave for life.

Though less dramatically, and perhaps even unknowingly, we have also gone through this name-changing/identity-changing process. In Jeremiah 1:5 we get an awesome revelation that human beings are individually designed and assigned by God himself to fulfill purpose and destiny within the Earth. For Jeremiah it was to be a prophet; for me it was to be a Pastor and Bishop; for you it might be any number of spiritual or professional vocations. Acts 10:34 says, "God is no respecter of persons," so that means if God created Jeremiah with purpose, he created you with purpose. I assure you that purpose was *not* to be a slave.

The Bible teaches that God puts gifts and resources within us and around us to be successful, and to reach our God-given potential and purpose. Let me reinforce my point, just to help you understand what I am saying. Revelation 1:6 informs us that when you came into Christ, you and I were made Kings and Priests unto God.

And hath made us kings and priests unto God and his Father; to him be glory and dominion for ever and ever. Amen.

(Revelation 1:6)

That's right, you and I are now Kings, just like the book of 2 Corinthians teaches; when we come into Christ, "We are a new creature." God did a new work in your life so that you can have all and be all the scriptures say that you can be. Unfortunately, many of us have been living as Toby (enslaved to poverty, debt, or lack) so long that we don't know how to be Kunta anymore. We are like the Children of Israel on their way to the Promised Land, unwilling to live by faith to receive the promise, and longing to return to Egypt.

There is also the account in Numbers 13 that brings to light this mental struggle for identity. Even when the Children of Israel reach the Promised Land, before they can go in they have to overcome their identity crises. They are unable to identify themselves as the Children of the Promise and heirs to King of Kings as God says they are. Instead, even after seeing how good the Promised Land is and knowing that God himself has promised it to them, they see themselves as unworthy and unable to possess it. The after-effects of slavery clouded their view of themselves.

And they told him, and said, **We came unto the land** whither thou sentest us, and **surely it floweth with milk and honey**; and this is the fruit of it. Nevertheless the people be strong that dwell in the land, and the cities are walled, and very great: and moreover we saw the children of Anak there. The Amalekites dwell in the land of the south: and the Hittites, and the Jebusites, and the Amorites, dwell in the mountains: and the Canaanites dwell by the sea, and by the coast of Jordan.   *Numbers 13:27-29*

But the men that went up with him said, "We be not able to go up against the people; for they are stronger than we." And **they brought up an evil report of the land which they had searched** unto the children of Israel, saying, "The land, through which we have gone to search it, is a land that eateth up the inhabitants thereof; and all the people that we saw in it are men of a great stature. And there we saw the giants, the sons of Anak, which come of the giants: and **we were in our own sight as grasshoppers**, and **so we were in their sight.**"

Numbers 13:31-33

This story clearly indicates the mental

struggle that many Children of God suffer. In this passage, the Children of Israel actually reached the Promised Land. They sent out 12 spies to scout out the land to make sure it was the place. Even though they were convinced it was the place they were promised (verse 27)-- "sure [this is the place] it flows with milk and honey," they felt they couldn't possess it. The other surrounding verses give a long list of reasons (excuses) why they felt they could take the land, but the most telling reason is in verse 33: **"we were in our own sight as grasshoppers."** They saw themselves as unworthy and inferior. Therefore, they assumed that the other people saw them the same way, "and **so we were in their sight**." The remarkable thing about it was that it was all in their mind. They were spies who sneaked in and out of the land. The other people never saw them, but they made up their own mind how others would see them based on how they saw themselves.

In verse 31 we see one who has a different mindset and rallies the people to go forth

Bishop Charles A. Messenger

and immediately take the land.

And Caleb stilled the people before Moses, and said, **Let us go up at once, and possess it; for we are well able to overcome it.**

Numbers 13:30

The key to this mindset is in the first few words: "And Caleb stilled the people." Child of God, if you're going to think like God and take what He has promised you, then you've got to still yourself. Psalms 46:10 says, "*Be still*, and know that I am God..." Still your fears, anxieties, and all negative thoughts and voices that tell you that you can't. You have got to believe and confess like Caleb, "I am well able to overcome it." I can take, have, get, and receive everything that God says that I can. God wants us, His children, to have the best, but we have been in slavery so long that many people have lost their taste for fine things.

If we are going to return to our royal status, our Kunta-ness where we identify ourselves as the princely children of the King of Kings, we have to embrace the divine purpose God has created us for. There are several essential things that a king must have:

A Kingdom – A place where the King rules, gives directions, and sets order.

But seek ye first the kingdom of God, and his righteousness; and all these things shall be added unto you. *(Matthew 6:33)*

Identify an actual geographical location where the will and the kingdom system can be carried out. This can be a home, business, church, or land that is owned and controlled by the king.

A Royal Treasury – Money to Fund Kingdom Activities.

In the area of finances you have to understand that your finances and Kingdom finances are the same. In order for the Kingdom of God to have something, the people of God must first have that something. We need to understand that there is no money in Heaven. That's right; there isn't one Benjamin, one Grant, one Jackson or even a good ol' honest Abe Lincoln in Heaven. In order for financial needs to be met, projects to be financed, and finances to be used to fund visions for the Kingdom of God, we are going to have to raise the finances necessary to bring them to pass.

You and I are going to have to accept and operate in our roles as Kings on the Earth. Revelation 1:6 and 5:10 tell us that God has called us "kings and priests." Most believers have no problem seeing themselves as priests (holy, spiritual, light and salt) on the earth. We understand and gladly accept our calling to be the spiritual representatives of God on the Earth. However, most of us don't have a clue that we are called to be kings, much less know *how* to be kings. That is what this whole book has been about–developing a Kingdom Mindset and putting ourselves in position, through operating in Kingdom Principles, so that we receive financial blessings and reap a bountiful financial harvest. This will enable us to live out the Abrahamic covenant of **being blessed to be a blessing.**

In the Old Testament we see kings like David who would go to war, defeat the enemy, and bring back the spoils (wealth, riches, and money) into their kingdom. That is our same role today. Rather than fight on the battlefield of some foreign country, we are to fight on the battlefield of industry and commerce. Our jobs, businesses, and the investment arenas are where we are to do battle and bring back the spoils into the kingdom. We have to understand that we have been unbalanced in our pursuit of the kingdom. Everyone has sought after the spiritual in-house ministry pursuits.

We limit ministry to singing in the choir, being a praise dancer, preaching the word, and other "priestly things". But we fail to understand that being successful in industry and the marketplace is an essential calling as well. If we look at the Nation of Israel [Biblical People of God], they were divided into 12 tribes, and out of the 12 tribes only one tribe (Levi-the smallest tribe) was dedicated to the priestly order. On top of that, if we do the math, we'll find out that numerically this means that only one out of 20 was called to function in the priestly order; the rest were called to the kingly order to help build and expand the Kingdom. With this in mind, you and I had better understand that we have to get busy operating like kings.

FAITH SUMMARY

God has set Kings in place to have dominion over this earth. These kings can not allow the rulers of the world to strip them of their divine name and authority (Kunta). You are a King. When you come to understand what that truly means, you will start walking as God's King. To some degree every believer has a place to establish that kingdom system of God; a home, business, church etc... it's time for you to reject the influence of this world and walk as Kunta and not as Tobi.

The Proverbs 22:7 says, "The rich rule over the poor and the borrower is servant to the lender." God don't wont you to be a slave to anyone or anything. You are a King so it's time you start acting like it.

Practical Examples of Wealth Creation and Money Management

Up until now, I have given you a lot of Word and Spiritual Insights. Before I leave you, I want to give you some practical things you need to do to complement what I've been teaching you.

Eliminate debt and get out of slavery.

You have to face the giant. I will give you practical ways to get out of your debt situation. These are things that help me and my wife get out of debt and the death that comes with it. Truth is, you aren't the only one hurting from the sting of overwhelming debt, many people around the world are experiencing its weight.

BE PRACTICAL

These practical steps that I will share with you are powerful beyond words. If you follow them they will lift you out of debt. Can you see a life without debt? These are practical strategies can help you come out of your debt situation. Putting God into your situation by giving will cause you to come out faster.

1. ### Write it down and make it plan

You have to write down how much debt you're in right now. You've got to find where you are. Don't be afraid; once you know the number you can plan your way out. Remember you are not in this alone, god is with you every step of the way.

Writing it down for some people can be difficult. In fact, it can cause anxiety and depression. Yet if you want to get out of the valley of the shadow of death, you have to write it down. The Lord answered the prophet Habakkuk in Habakkuk 2.2, *"Write the vision and make it plain on tablets..."*. Once you have done that it's time to move to the next step of debt release.

1. Pay what you owe

The next practical thing to do is, eliminate the debt that has the highest interest first. You are breaking the super-natural cycle that has kept you bound. Bankers and creditors don't won't you to hear this, because they know that if people are freed from debt they are less likely to become bound in the future.

Next, put your bills in groups. One group we can call, Long-term, the other Mid-term, and Short-term. Each group should be organized from the highest interest to the lowest.

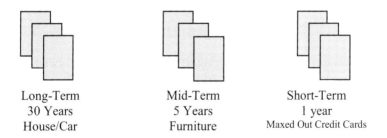

Long-Term	Mid-Term	Short-Term
30 Years	5 Years	1 year
House/Car	Furniture	Maxed Out Credit Cards

Now start with the Short-term group and chose the bill that has the fasted growing interest. Continue to make payments on the other bills but only pay the minimum. Use the extra cash flow from the other bills to pay off the high interest bills.

Yet do not stop paying your tithe and offering. You want God in this situation. When you pay your tithe and sow your seed, you cause God to bring super-natural favor in your life. If you try to do this on your own it will take forever. You can't x God out of your money. You need Him there more than ever.

After you have paid off your Short-term group go on to your Mid-term group and follow the same principle. After awhile, your credit score will rise, and you will have more cash flow.

3. <u>Spend less than you make</u>

Learn to live below your means. For most people this will take practice, practice, and more practice. Yet don't give up, if you faint not you will reap a harvest.

Money management is not about how

much you make; it's how much you keep. How much you make will increase with giving. If you are swimming in debt and dodging creditors, you have to stop and realize what you are doing isn't working. These principles worked for me and my family. Spending more than what we had was foolishness. It's time to walk wiser. Credit cards need to be used wisely. They should not be used to spend what you don't have yet, especially not daily.

4. <u>Start Investing</u>

After you are faithful to the above principles you will start to see more cash-flow. What you do with this is important. Once you start accumulating some savings, you need to (with good financial advice) start investing. Make sure you diversify. Look for short-term, mid-term and long-term investments. I must add, do not x God from your financial planning. The best investment to make is to sow into the kingdom of God. You will win every time.

When you have more money and you are

faithful to God, opportunities will come your way. Of course be careful, don't jump in the bed with every great idea that comes across your desk. Pray and ask God and your mentors for advice and direction.

5. <u>Learn how to cut corners</u>

True money management skills happen when you learn how to be wise about what you want and how to get it. Sure there are many name brand products and let's be honest most people can't live without their name brand items. Yet, with a little research on the web you can find the same value in a non-name brand item.

When you have set your faith to get out of debt you have to make some sacrifices. However you don't have to sacrifice value. That's what people have to understand. Name brand don't always mean value. For example, Crest tooth paste is a name brand tooth-paste that is common in most households. Yet when you do your research you will find that Ultra-bright has faired the same or better than Crest in most studies. In addition, Ultra Bright is half the price. Shopping wisely is something that takes a little research but the time and effort you spend can save you hundreds of dollars a month.

Here are some other tips for cutting corners and saving you money. When you go grocery shopping make a list of the things you need before the things you want. I know it sounds simple, but these are the strategies that have made my wife and I millionaires. Sure you might do it a little different. For example my friend uses a cell phone app to compile his shopping list. The grocery store's mission is to make you spend more money than you planned. It is set up to make you spend.

Don't always take the kids to the store with you. Children have a way of making parents spend more than they planned. Now if your children are disciplined and can stick to the plan than let them help. Otherwise, leave them at home. Going to the grocery store when you are hungry is another common mistake. You will automatically have to have everything you see. When you get home and start unpacking bags you will find that you didn't get anything to make big meals that last a few days. Also I know you may want to buy clothing for you and the family. So don't try to do this all at once, big mistake. Plan your spending. Buy a couple of shirts this weekend and a pair of shoes in a couple weeks. If you have a regular job you can easy plan when you can buy a few items.

Oh, let's not forget to take coupons. Also look for discounts and sales. You have to become a sale vulture. Write down the stores that you frequent and get to know the workers. They can let you in on hot tips about upcoming sales and discounts. Also the internet is full of coupon websites that help you buy even name brand items.

Lastly, discount stores are a growing market in the United States. You have to learn where they are in your town or city. If you normally shop at upscale stores like Lund's and Barley's where there is a higher mark up of items, you may have to consider Aldi's or Wal-mart. These stores mission is to help you get more for less. Also, instead of Blockbuster and Domino's, get yourself a pizza from Rainbow or Cub and a Redbox movie. It won't hurt your bank as much as other premium choices.

FAITH SUMMARY

Learning to be frugal may cause some short-term discomfort, but it will lead to long-term success. When you do it God's way, the blessings will find you and overtake you. Pastors and ministers and fellow workers, remember to make people your focus. Talking about money is just a type of fishing. Jesus said, "I'm going to teach you to be fishers of men." Everyone following Jesus wasn't following because they liked his preaching. Yet, most of them wanted miracles, fishes and loaves. To catch fish you must have bait. What's your bait? Are the fish biting? If not, change your bait or your fishing hole. *The money is in the fish's mouth... the people are the fish.*

Learn to be wiser about managing your life and money. If you are a good faith student and steward you will eat the good, and have some to share. When you exercise wisdom and good stewardship, God will maximize your efforts and cause you to be more effective at your life and ministry.

.